Storm Clou

GW01398764

E. E. Smith

Alpha Editions

This edition published in 2024

ISBN : 9789362927330

Design and Setting By
Alpha Editions
www.alphaedis.com
Email - info@alphaedis.com

CHAPTER ONE
FROM A SEED....

Tellurian Pharmaceuticals, Inc., was civilization's oldest and most conservative drug house. "Hide-bound" was the term most frequently used, not only by its younger employees but also by its more progressive competitors. But, corporatively, Tellurian Pharmaceuticals did not care. Its board of directors, by an iron-clad, if unwritten law, was limited to men of over three score years and ten.

Against the inertia of that ruling body the impetuosity of the younger generations was precisely as efficacious as the dashing of waves against the foot of an adamantine cliff—and in very much the same fashion. Ocean waves do, in time, cut into even the hardest rock; and, every century or so, Tellurian Pharmaceutical, Inc., did take a forward step. However, "Rather than make a mistake, do nothing" was its creed. To that creed it adhered rigorously.

Thus, it did not establish branches upon other planets until a century or so of experiment had proved that no unforeseen factor would operate to lessen the prodigiously high standard of its products. Nor would it own or operate spaceships, as did other large firms. Its business was the manufacture of the universe's finest, most carefully standardized drugs and it would go into no sidelines whatever.

Even the location of its head office; directly under the guns of Prime Base, bore out the same theme. Originally it had been in the middle of the city, miles away from the reservation; but as Prime Base had expanded, the city had moved aside. Tellurian Pharmaceuticals, however, would not give way. It stolidly refused to sell its holdings even to the Galactic Patrol; it would not move until the patrol should condemn its property and compel it by law to vacate.

Into that massive gray building there strode a tall, lean, gray man; into an old-fashioned elevator, operated by a seventy-year-old "boy"; into a darkish, severe room whose rock-of-ages furniture had become pricelessly antique. Without a word he handed a card to the receptionist, a prim spinster of some fifty summers.

"Ezekiel R. Stonely, M.D., Sc.D., Consultant in Radiation," she read precisely into a communicator. "By appointment."

"Let him come in, please."

Dr. Stonely entered the private office of a vice-president—a young man, as T. P.'s executives went—a man scarcely sixty years of age.

"All ready," the consultant reported briefly. "Graves is here, you said?"

"Yes. He got in from Deka last night. How long will the demonstration take?"

"Seven hours to the point of maximum yield; twelve for the full life cycle."

"Very good." The vice-president then spoke into the communicator. "Please ask Mr. Graves to step in."

Graves, the manager of T. P.'s branch upon the planet Deka— planetographically speaking, Dekanore III—was a short, fat man; and he possessed, upon the surface at least, the fat man's proverbial geniality and good nature.

"Mr. Graves—Dr. Stonely."

"Mighty glad to meet you, Doctor," Graves shook hands effusively. "Splendid accomplishment. You've been working on it five years or more, I hear."

"Six years and two months," the scientist said precisely.

"I cannot accompany you, of course," the vice-president interposed busily, "and you appreciate that the less of communication or contact hereafter, the better. Good day."

The two went out, took a cab, and soon were in Dr. Stonely's ultra-private laboratory. It was a large room, artificially lighted, lined throughout with sheet metal—metal which, when properly charged, formed a barrier through which no harmful radiation or particle could pass. The scientist snapped on the wall shield and set to work, explaining each step to his visitor.

"Here are the seeds. For the present you will have to take my word for it that I produced them here. I will go through as many cycles as you please. Here are the containers—miniatures, you will observe, of the standard hydroponics tanks. The formula of the nutrient solution, while of course crucial, contains nothing either rare or unduly expensive. I plant the seed, thus, in each of the two tanks. I cover each with a bell-jar of plastic— transparent to the frequencies to be employed. I enclose the whole with a similar envelope—so. I align the projectors—thus. We will now put on our armor, as the radiation is severe and the atmosphere, which displaces our own of oxygen—"

"Synthetic or imported?" Graves asked.

"Imported. Synthesis is possible, but prohibitive in cost. Importation in tank ships is easy, simple, and comparatively cheap. I will now energize the projectors, and growth will begin."

He did so, and in the glare of blue-green radiance the atmosphere within the bell-jars, the very ether, warped and writhed. In spite of the distortion of vision, however, growth could be perceived—growth at an astonishing rate.

In a few minutes the seeds had sprouted. In an hour the thick, broad, glossily-green leaves were inches long. In seven hours each jar was full of a lushly luxuriant tangle of foliage.

"This is the point of maximum yield," Stonely remarked as he shut off the projectors. "I assume that you will want to take a sample."

"Certainly," the fat man agreed. "How else would I know it's the clear quill?"

"If you were a scientist, the sight of it would be sufficient," came the dry rejoinder. "Knowing that you are not, however, I am running two tanks, as you see. Take either one you like."

The sample tank was removed and the full cycle of growth completed upon the other. Graves himself harvested the seeds, and himself carried them away.

Six days, six generations, six samples, and even the eminently skeptical Graves was convinced.

"You've certainly got something there, Doc," he admitted finally. "We can really go to town on that. You're absolutely sure that you're covered—no trace?"

"None whatever," Stonely assured him. "Doctor Stonely will retire and will gradually drop from sight. I will abandon this disguise, resume my true identity as Fairchild, which has been kept alive judiciously, and move openly to Deka."

"Notes? Data? Possible observers? This machinery and stuff?" Graves insisted.

"No notes or data have ever been written down. The knowledge exists only in my own brain. You are the first person other than myself ever to see the inside of this room. This apparatus will be unrecognizable before it is boxed, and I shall do the packing myself. Why? Are you by any chance apprehensive that I may slip up?"

"Well, we can't be too sure." The fat man's blue eyes were now neither genial nor good-natured; they were piercing and cold. "In this game anybody who permits any leaks dies. And anyone who knows too much dies. We don't want you to die, at least until after we get started on Deka—"

"Nor then," the scientist interrupted cynically, "if you know when you're well off. I'm the only man in the universe who can run the apparatus. It would take a mighty good man three years to learn it after I get it going. Remember that, my friend."

"So what?" Graves' stare was coldly level.

"Just so you won't develop any funny ideas. I know as well as you do, however, about leaks and leakers. I don't leak. How long will it take you to get ready—three months?"

"Um—just about. And you?"

"Any time."

"Make it three months, then."

"Three months it is—on Deka." The interview was ended.

Newspoke—originally New Spokane—was the largest city of Dekanore III. It lay in the broad valley of the Spokane River, just above the mouth of Clear Creek, which latter stream meandered along a fertile valley between mountains lofty and steep. Clear Creek Valley—all of it—and all its neighboring mountains belonged to Tellurian Pharmaceuticals, Inc.

The valley floor was a riot of color, devoted as it was to the intensive cultivation of medicinal plants which could not as yet be grown economically in tanks. Along both edges of the valley extended rows of huge hydroponics sheds. Upon the mountains' sides there were snake dens, lizard pens, and enclosures for many other species of fauna.

Nor was the surface all that was in use. Those mountains were hollow, honeycombed into a host of rooms in which, under precisely controlled environments of temperature, atmosphere, and radiation, were grown and studied hundreds of widely-variant forms of life.

At the confluence of creek and river, just inside the city limits, there reared and sprawled the company's buildings, the processing and synthesizing plants, the refineries, the laboratories, the power-houses, and so on.

In a ground-floor office of the towering Administration Building two men sat in silence and waited while a red light upon a peculiarly complicated desk-board faded through pink into pure white.

"All clear. This way, Doctor." Manager Graves pushed a button and a section of blank wall slid smoothly aside.

The fat man and Doctor Fairchild—unrecognizable now as the man who had once been known as Doctor Stonely—went down two long flights of narrow steps. Along a dimly-lit corridor they made their way, through an elaborately locked steel door, then into a barely-furnished, steel-lined room upon the floor of which four inert bodies lay.

Graves thrust a key into an inconspicuous orifice and a plate swung open, revealing a chute into which the four lax forms were unceremoniously dumped. Then the two men retraced their steps to the manager's office.

"Well, that's about all that we can feed to the disintegrators." Fairchild lit an Alsakanite cigarette and exhaled thoughtfully.

"Why? Going soft on us?" Graves sneered.

"No," the scientist replied calmly. "The ice is getting thin."

"Whaddya mean 'thin'?" the manager demanded. "The Patrol inspectors are ours—enough of them, anyway. Our records are fixed. Faked identities, trips, all that stuff, you know. Everything's on the green."

"That's what you think," Fairchild countered cynically. "Our accident rate, in spite of everything we have been able to do, is up three hundredths of one percent; industrial hazard rate and employee turnover about three and a half; and the Narcotics Division alone knows how much we have upped total bootleg sales. Those figures are all in the Patrol's files. How can you give such facts the brush-off?"

"We don't have to," Graves laughed comfortably. "Even a half of one percent would not excite suspicion, and our distribution is so uniform throughout the galaxy that they can't center it. They can't possibly trace anything back to us. Besides, they wouldn't suspect us. With our reputation, other firms would get knocked off in time to give us plenty of warning. Lutzenschiffer's, for instance, is putting out heroin by the ton."

"Again I say that's what *you* think." Fairchild remained entirely unconvinced. "Nobody else is putting out the stuff that comes out of Cave Two Seventeen—demand and price prove that. What you don't seem to get, Graves, is that some of those damned Lensmen have brains. Suppose they put Worsel of Velantia, Tregonsee of Rigel IV, or even Kinnison himself onto this job—then what? The minute that anybody decides to run a rigid statistical analysis of our records, we're done."

"Um—" This was a distinctly disquieting thought, in view of the impossibility of concealing anything from a Gray Lensman who was really on the prowl. "That might not be so good. What would you advise, then?"

"Shut down Two Seventeen—and preferably the whole hush-hush end—until we can get our records absolutely honest and our death rates down to the old-time ten-year average," the scientist insisted. "In that way only can we make ourselves really safe."

"Shut down? The way they're pushing us for production?" Graves sneered. "You talk like a fool. The chief would toss us both down the chute and put somebody in here that *would* really produce."

"Oh, I don't mean without permission. Talk him into it. It's best for him, as well as everybody else, over the long pull."

"He couldn't see it. I can't either, really," grunted the manager. "If we can't dope out something better than that, things have got to go on as is."

"I suspected so—but you asked me. The next best thing is to use some new form of death, openly explainable, to clean up our books."

"Wonderful!" Graves snorted contemptuously. "What can we possibly add to what we are using right along?"

"A loose atomic vortex."

"Whoooosh!" The fat man deflated in an exclamation of profound surprise, then came back up for air, gasping. "Man, you're nuts. There's only one on the planet, and it's—or do you mean—but nobody ever touched one of those things off deliberately! Can it be done?"

"Yes. It isn't simple, but we Fellows of the College of Radiation know how—theoretically—the transformation can be made to occur. The fact that it is a new idea makes it all the better. It has never been done because it has been impossible to extinguish the things. But now 'Storm' Cloud is putting them out."

"I see. Neat, very neat." Graves' agile and cunning brain was going over the possibilities. "Certain of our employees, I take it, will be upon a picnic in the upper end of the valley when this unfortunate occurrence is to take place?"

"Exactly—and enough mythical ones to straighten out our bookkeeping. Then, later, we can dispose of suspects as they appear. Vortices are absolutely unpredictable, you know. People we don't like can die of radiation or of any one or a mixture of various toxic gases and vapors and the vortex will take the blame."

"And later, when it gets dangerous, Storm Cloud can blow it out for us," Graves gloated. "But we'll not want him for a long, long time!"

"No, but we'll report it and ask for him the hour it happens—" Fairchild silenced the manager's expostulations. "Use your head, Graves! Anybody who has a vortex go out of control wants it killed as soon as possible. But here's the joker—Cloud has enough Class A prime urgent demands on file right now to keep him busy for the next ten or fifteen years. Therefore we won't be able to get him—see?"

"I see. This is nice, Fairchild, very, very nice. But the head office had better keep an eye on Cloud, just the same."

CHAPTER TWO
VORTEX BUSTER

Robert Ryder, Bachelor of Hydroponics from the University of Newspoke, was also, maritally, a bachelor. For a year or so after graduation, while he was making good with Tellurian Pharmaceutical, Inc., he had no reason to be dissatisfied with that state of affairs. However, Mother Nature went to work upon him in her wonted fashion, and, never averse to feminine society, he began to go in for girls in a large and serious way.

In the hydroponics office there was an eminently personable and yet level-headed young filing clerk named Jacqueline Comstock, who was all unconsciously—or was it?—working much more toward her Mrs. degree than for the good of the firm.

It was inevitable, then, that these two should single each other out; that each should come to behold in the other all that made life worth while. They planned, breathtakingly happy.

They saved their money, instead of indulging in expensive amusements; they took long hikes.

Thus they discovered many choice spots affording the maximum of privacy, of comfort, and of view; thus they came to know almost as individuals the birds and beasts and reptiles in the far-flung pens.

They sat blissfully, arms around each other, upon a rustic seat improvised from rocks, branches, and leaves. Below them, almost under their feet, was a den of venomous serpents, but they did not see the snakes.

Before them, equally unperceived, there extended the magnificent vista of stream and valley and mountain.

All they saw, however, was each other—until their attention was literally wrenched to a man who was climbing frantically toward them with the aid of a stout cudgel which he used as a staff. The girl gazed briefly, stared, and then, with a half-articulate moan, shrank even closer against her lover's side. Ryder, even while his left arm tightened around his Jackie's waist, felt with his right hand for a club of his own and tensed his muscles in readiness for strife—for the climbing man was all too apparently mad.

His breathing was horrible. Mouth tight-clamped, in spite of his terrific exertion, he was sniffing—sniffing loathsomely, lustfully, each whistling inhalation filling his lungs to bursting. He exhaled explosively, as though begrudging the second of time required to empty himself of air. Wide-open eyes glaring fixedly ahead, he blundered upward, paying no attention whatever to his path. He tore through clumps of thorny growth; he stumbled and fell over logs and stones; he caromed from boulders, as careless of the needles which tore clothing and skin as of the rocks which bruised his flesh to the very bone.

He struck the gate of the pen immediately beneath the two appalled watchers, and then stopped. He moved to the right and paused, whimpering in anxious agony. Back to the gate and over to the left he went, where he stopped and sent forth a blood-curdling howl. Whatever the frightful compulsion was, whatever it was that he sought, he could not deviate enough from his line to go around the pen. He looked, and for the first time saw the gate and the fence and the ophidian inhabitants of the den. They did not matter—nothing mattered. He fumbled with the lock, then furiously attacked it and the gate and the fence with his club—fruitlessly. He tried to climb the fence, but failed. He tore off sandals and socks and, by dint of thrusting fingers and toes ruthlessly into the narrow meshes of the woven wire, he succeeded in getting through.

No more than he had minded the thorns and the rocks did he mind the eight strands of viciously-barbed wire surmounting that fence. He did, however, watch the snakes. He took pains to drop into an area temporarily clear of them, and he pounded to death the half-dozen serpents bold enough to bar his path.

Then, dropping to the ground, he writhed and scuttled about, sniffing ever harder, nose plowing the ground. He halted; he dug with his bare hands at the hard soil. Thrusting his face into the hole, he inhaled tremendously. His body writhed, trembled, shuddered uncontrollably, then stiffened convulsively into a supremely ecstatic rigidity, terrible to gaze upon.

The horribly labored breathing ceased. The body collapsed bonelessly, even before the outraged serpents crawled up and struck.

Jacqueline Comstock saw very little of the outrageous performance. She screamed once, shut both eyes and, twisting about within the embracing arm, burrowed her face into the man's left shoulder.

Ryder, however—white-faced, jaw set, sweating—watched the whole ghastly thing to its grimly cataclysmic end. When it was over he licked his lips and swallowed hard before he could talk.

"It's all over, dear—no danger now," he finally managed to say. "We'd better go. We ought to turn in an alarm—make a report or something. They'll want us as witnesses."

"Oh, I can't, Bob!" she sobbed. "If I open my eyes I just know I'll look, and if I look I'll ... I'll just simply turn inside out."

"Hold everything, Jackie! Keep your eyes shut. I'll pilot you and tell you when it's safe to look."

More than half carrying his companion, still gripping unconsciously his heavy club, the man set off down the rugged trail. Out of sight of what had happened, the girl opened her eyes and they continued the descent in a more usual, more decorous fashion until they met a man hurrying upwards.

"Oh, Doctor Fairchild! There was a—" But the report which Ryder was about to make was unnecessary; the alarm had already been given.

"I know!" the scientist puffed. "Stop! Stay right where you are." He jabbed a finger emphatically downward to anchor the couple in the exact spot they occupied. "Don't talk! Don't say a word—until I get back."

Fairchild returned after a time, unhurried and completely at ease. He did not need to ask the shaken couple if they had seen what had occurred. It was plainly evident that they had.

"But—but, Doctor—" Ryder began.

"Keep still! Don't talk at all!" Fairchild ordered brusquely. Then, in an ordinary conversational tone, he went on: "Until we have investigated this extraordinary occurrence thoroughly—sifted it to the bottom—the probability of spying cannot be disregarded. As the only eye-witnesses to what actually happened, your reports will be exceedingly valuable. But I do not want to hear a word until we are in a place which I am sure beyond peradventure is proof against any and all spy-rays. Do you understand?"

"Oh yes, I understand."

"Pull yourselves together, then. Act unconcerned, casual—particularly when we get to the Administration Building. Talk about the weather, or, better yet, about the honeymoon you are going to take on Chickladoria."

Thus it was that there was nothing noticeably abnormal about the group of three which strolled into the office building and entered a private automatic elevator. The conveyance, however, went down instead of up.

"I am taking you to my private laboratory, not to my office," Fairchild replied to Ryder's unspoken question. "Frankly, young folks, I am a scared—a badly scared man."

This statement, so true and yet so misleading, resolved thoroughly the young engineer's inchoate doubts. Entirely unsuspectingly the couple accompanied the Senior Radiationist along the grim corridor. They paused as he unlocked and swung open a door of thick metal; they stepped unquestioningly into the room in response to his gestured invitation. He did not, however, follow them. Instead, he swung shut the heavy slab, whose closing cut off completely the filing clerk's piercing scream of fear.

"Cut out that noise!" came raspingly from a speaker in the steel ceiling of the small room—a room which was very evidently not Doctor Fairchild's private laboratory. "It won't do you any good. You're sound-proofed. Talk all you please, but any more of that yelling and I'll have to put you out of your misery."

"But Mr. Graves, I thought—Dr. Fairchild told us—we were to report on that—" Ryder's words came confusedly from the maze of his surprise.

"You're to report on nothing. You saw too much and know too much, that's all."

"Oh, so *that's* it." Ryder's mind reeled as some part of the actual significance of what he had seen struck home. "But listen, Graves. Jackie didn't see anything. She had her eyes shut all the time, and doesn't know anything. You don't want the murder of such a girl as she is on your mind, I know. Let her go and she'll never say a word. We'll both swear to that. Or you could—"

"Why? Just because she's got a face and a shape?" the fat man sneered. "There are thousands of women as good-looking as she is, but I've got only one life—" Graves broke off as Fairchild entered the office.

"Well, how about it? How bad is it?" the manager asked.

"Not bad at all. Everything's under control."

"Listen, Doctor Fairchild!" Ryder put in, desperately, "surely you don't have to murder Jackie here in cold blood. I was just suggesting to Graves that he could get a therapist—"

"Shut up," the scientist ordered coldly. "Our therapists are working on things that are really important. You two must die."

"But why?" Ryder protested wildly. He could not as yet perceive more than a small fraction of the whole. "I tell you, it's—"

"We'll let you guess," said Fairchild.

Shock upon shock had been too much for the girl's overstrained nerves. She fainted quietly and Ryder eased her unconscious form down to the cold steel floor.

"Can't you put her into a better place than this?" the man protested then.

"You'll find water and food, and that's enough." Graves laughed coarsely. "You won't live very long, so don't worry about conveniences. But keep still. If you want to know what is going to happen to you, listen—we have no objections to that—but one more word out of you and I cut the circuit. Go ahead, Fairchild, with what you were saying."

"There was a fault in the rock. Small, but big enough to let a little of the fine smoke seep through. He must have been a sniffer before to be able to smell the trace of the stuff that was drifting down the hill. All fixed now, though. I'm having the fault, and any others that may exist, cemented up solid. Death by snake bite will fix our records."

"Fair enough. Now, how about these two? There has been some talk of a honeymoon to Chickladoria, but that may have been a blind. Doubles? Disappearance? The vortex? What do you think?"

"Um—We've got to hold the risk at minimum." Fairchild pondered for minutes. "We can't disintegrate them, that's sure. We're trying to clear our books of too much of that stuff already. They've got to be found dead, and the quota for the vortex for this period is full. Therefore we'll have to keep them alive and out of sight—where they are is as good a place as any—for a week."

"Why alive? We've kept stiffs in storage before now."

"Too chancey—dead tissues change too much. We weren't courting investigation then, but now we are—on the vortex, at least—so we have to keep our noses clean. How about this? They decided that they couldn't wait any longer and got married today. You, big-hearted philanthropist that you are, told them that they could take their two weeks vacation immediately and that you would square it with their department heads. They went on their honeymoon. Not to Chickladoria, of course—too long and too risky—but to a place where nobody knows them. We can fake the evidence on that easily enough. They come back in about a week, to get settled, and the vortex gets them. See any flaws in that set-up?"

"No, that looks perfect," Graves decided after due deliberation. "One week from tonight, at midnight, they go out. Hear that, Ryder?"

"Yes, you pot-bellied—"

The fat man snapped a switch.

Doggedly and skillfully though he tried, Ryder could open up no avenue of escape or of communication; Fairchild and Graves had seen efficiently to that. And Jacqueline, in the inevitability of impending death, steadied down to meet it. She was a woman. In minor crises she had hidden her face and had shrieked and had fainted; but in this ultimate one she drew from the depths of her woman's soul not only a power to overcome her own weaknesses, but also an extra something with which to sustain and to fortify Ryder in his black moments.

They were together. That fact, and the far more important one that they were to die together, robbed incarceration and death itself of sting.

At the Atomic Research Laboratory on Teelus a conference was taking place between Unattached Lensmen Philip Strong, the head of that laboratory, and Doctor Neal Cloud, ex-atomic-physicist, now "Storm" Cloud, the Vortex Blaster.

Cloud had become the Vortex Blaster because a fragment of a loose atomic vortex had wiped out his entire family—not by coincidence, but by sheer cosmic irony. For he, while protecting his home and his loved ones from lightning by means of a mathematically infallible network of lightning rods, had all unknowingly erected a super-powerful magnet for loose-flying vortices of atomic disintegration.

Nor were such vortices scarce. Every time an atomic powerplant went out of control, a loose atomic vortex resulted, and there was, at that time, no way of extinguishing them. It was theoretically possible to blow them out with duodec, but the charge of explosive had to match within very close limits the instantaneous value of the vortex's activity. Since that value varied rapidly and almost unpredictably, practically all such attempts resulted in the death of the operator and the creation of a dozen or more new centers of annihilation.

There was a possibility that Cloud, a mathematical prodigy able to compute instantaneously any mathematical problem, would be able to succeed where so many others had failed; but as long as he had Jo and the three kids, as long as he had the normal love of life, that possibility had never occurred to him.

When he lost them, however, he no longer had the slightest interest in living. Unwilling to kill himself, he decided to try to blow out the oldest and worst vortex upon Tellus. Against the orders of his chief and the pleadings of his friends he tried it. He succeeded.

He had been burned; he had been broken, but he carried no scars. The Phillips treatment for the replacement of lost or damaged members of the human body had taken care of that. His face looked youthful; his hard-schooled, resiliently responsive body was in startlingly fine condition for that of a man of forty.

The Phillips treatment could not, however, fill a dully aching void within him. It could not eradicate from mind and soul the absence of and the overpowering longing for his deceased wife and children—particularly his wife, Jo the lovely, Jo the beloved, Jo his all in all for eighteen fleeting and intensely happy years.

He no longer wore that psychic trauma visibly; it no longer came obtrusively between him and those with whom he worked, but it was and always would be there. He had by this time blown out so many vortices and had developed such an effective technique that he no longer had any hope that any vortex could ever kill him—but there were other forms of death. He still would not actually court it; but more and more certainly, as the days dragged on, he came to know that not by one single millimeter would he dodge anyone or anything bringing the dread messenger his way.

"Where do you want me to go next, Chief?" the Vortex Blaster asked. "Spica or Rigel or Corvina? Those three are the worst, I'd say."

"Uh-huh—Rigel's is probably a shade the worst in property damage and urgency. Before we decide, though, I wish you'd take a good look at the data on this one from Dekanore III. See if you see what I do."

"Dekanore III?" Cloud glanced curiously at the older man. "Didn't know they were having any trouble. Only got one, haven't they?"

"Two now—they just had a new one. It's that new one I'm talking about. It's acting funny—damned funny."

Cloud went through the data in brow-furrowing concentration, then charted some of it and frowned.

"I get it. 'Damned funny' is right," he agreed. "The toxicity is too steady, but at the same time the composition of the effluvium seems to be too varied. Inconsistent, apparently—but since there's no real attempt at a gamma analysis and very little actual mathematical data, it could be; they're so utterly unpredictable. Inexperienced observers, I take it, with chemical and medical bias?"

"Very much so, from our angle."

"Well, I'll say this much—I never saw a gamma chart that would fit this stuff, and I can't even imagine what the sigma curve would look like. Boss, I'd like to run a full test on that baby before it goes orthodox."

"My thought exactly. And we have a valid excuse for giving it priority, too. It happens to be killing more people than all three of those bad ones combined."

"I can fix that toxicity, I think, with exciters; and I'll throw a solid cordon around it, if I have to, to keep the fools from getting themselves burned to death. However, I won't blow it out until I find out why it's acting so—if it is. Clear the ether, Chief, I'm practically there!"

It did not take long to load Cloud's apparatus-packed flitter into a liner, Dekanore-bound. But that trip was not uneventful. Half-way there an alarm rang out and the dread word "Pirates!" resounded throughout the ship.

Consternation reigned, for organized piracy had vanished with the fall of the Council of Boskone. Treasure ships were either warships themselves or were escorted by warships. But this vessel was no treasure ship; she was only a passenger liner.

She had had little enough warning—her alert Communications Officer had sent out only a part of his first distress call when the blanketing interference closed down. The pirate—a first-class super-dreadnought—flashed up, and a heavy visual beam drove in.

"Go inert," came the tense command. "We are coming aboard."

"Are you crazy?" The liner's captain was surprised and disgusted, rather than alarmed. "If not, you've got the wrong ship. Everything we have aboard, including the ransom—if any—you can get for our passengers, wouldn't pay your expenses."

"You wouldn't know, of course, that you are carrying a package of Lonabarian jewelry, would you?" The question was elaborately skeptical.

"I know damned well that I'm not!"

"We'll take the package you *haven't* got, then!" The pirate snapped. "Go inert and open up, or I'll inert you with a needle-beam and open you up, compartment by compartment—like this." A narrow beam lashed out and expired. "That was through one of your cargo holds, just to show you that I mean business. The next one will be through your control room."

Resistance being out of the question, the liner went inert, and while the intrinsic velocities of the two vessels were being matched, the attacker issued further instructions.

"All officers are to be in the control room, all passengers in the main saloon. Everybody unarmed. Any person wearing arms or slow in obeying orders will be blasted."

Lines were rigged and space-suited men crossed the intervening void.

One squad went to the control room. Its leader, seeing that the Communications Officer was still trying to drive a call through the blanket, beamed him down without a word, then fused the entire communications panel. The captain and four or five other officers, maddened by this cold-blooded butchery, went for their guns and were butchered in turn.

A larger group—helmets thrown back for unimpeded vision, hands bared for instantaneous and accurate use of weapons—invaded the main saloon. Most of them went on through to perform previously assigned tasks, only a half dozen posting themselves to guard the passengers. One of these guards, a hook-nosed individual wearing consciously an aura of authority and dominance, spoke.

"Just take it easy, folks, and nobody will get hurt. If any of you have guns, don't go for them. That's a specialty that—" One of his DeLameters flamed briefly. Cloud's right arm vanished almost to the shoulder. The man behind him—what was left of him—dropped.

"Take it easy, I said," he went calmly on. "You can tie that arm up, fella, if you want to. It was in line with that guy who was trying in his slow way to pull a gun. You nurse over there, take him to the sick-bay and let them fix up his wing. If anybody stops you tell them Number One said to. Now the rest of you watch your step. I'll cut down every damn one of you that so much as looks like he wanted to start something."

They obeyed. They were very near the point of panic, but in view of what had happened no one dared to make the first move. The leniency displayed toward the wounded man also had a soothing effect.

In a few minutes the looting parties returned to the saloon.

"Did you get it, Six?"

"We got it. It was in the mail, like you said."

"The safe?"

"Sure. Wasn't much in it, but not bad, at that."

"QX. Control room! All done—let's go!"

The pirates backed away, their vessel disappeared, and its passengers rushed for their staterooms.

Then: "Doctor Cloud—Chief Pilot calling Doctor Cloud," the speaker announced.

"Cloud speaking."

"Report to the control room, please."

"Oh, excuse me—I didn't know that you were wounded," the officer apologized as he saw the Blaster's bandaged stump. "You had better go to bed."

"Doing nothing would only make it worse. Can I be of any help?"

"Do you know anything about communicators?"

"A little."

"Good. All our communications officers were killed and the sets—even those in the lifeboats—blasted. You can't do much with your left hand, of course, but you may be able to boss the job of rigging up a spare."

"I can do more than you think," Cloud grinned wryly. "It so happens that I'm left-handed. Give me a couple of technicians and we'll see what we can do."

They set to work, but before they had accomplished anything a cruiser drove up, flashing its identification as a warship of the Galactic Patrol.

"We picked up the partial call you got off," the young commander said briskly. "With that and the center of interference we didn't lose any time. Let's make this snappy." He was itching to be off after the marauder, but he could not leave until he had ascertained the facts and had been given a clearance signal by the merchantman's commanding officer. "You aren't hurt much. Don't need to call a repair-ship for you, do I?"

"No."

"QX." A quick investigation ensued.

"Anybody who ships stuff like that open mail ought to lose it, but it's tough on innocent bystanders. Anything else I can do for you?" the rescuer asked.

"Not unless you can lend us a communications officer or two."

"Sorry, but we're short-handed there ourselves. Can give you anybody else you need though, I think."

"Nothing else, thanks."

"Sign this clearance then, please, and I'll get on that fellow's tail. I'll send a copy of the report to your owners' head office. Clear ether!"

The visitor shot away and the liner, after repairs had been made, resumed its course toward Dekanore, with Cloud and a couple of electrical technicians as communications officers.

The Vortex Blaster was met effusively at the dock by Manager Graves himself. The fat man was overwhelmingly sorry that Cloud had lost his arm, but assured him that the accident wouldn't lay him up very long. He, Graves, would get a Posenian surgeon over here so fast that—

If the manager was taken aback to learn that Cloud had had a Phillips treatment already, he scarcely showed it. He escorted the specialist to Deka's best hotel, where he introduced him largely and volubly. Graves took him to supper. Graves took him to a theater and showed him the town. Graves told the hotel management to give the specialist the best rooms and the best valet they had and that all of his activities whatever their nature, purpose, or extent, were to be charged to Tellurian Pharmaceuticals, Inc. Graves was a grand guy.

Cloud broke loose finally, however, and went to the dock to see about storing his flitter.

It had not been unloaded. There would be a slight delay, he was informed, because of the insurance inspections necessitated by the damage—and Cloud had not known that there had been any damage! When he had found out just what that beam had done to his little ship he swore viciously and sought out the liner's Chief Pilot.

"Why didn't you tell me that that damned pirate holed us?" he demanded hotly.

"Why didn't you ask?" the officer replied, honestly surprised. "I don't suppose that it occurred to anybody—I know it didn't to me—that you might be interested."

And that was, Cloud knew, strictly true. Passengers were not informed of such occurrences. He had been enough of an officer so that he could have learned everything if he had so wished, but not enough of one to have been informed of such matters as routine. Nor was it surprising that it had not come up in conversation. Damage to cargo meant nothing whatever to those in the liner's control room; a couple of easily-patched holes in the hull were not worth mentioning. From their standpoint the only real damage was done to the communicators, and Cloud himself had set them to rights. No, this delay was his own fault as much as anybody else's.

"You won't lose anything, though," the pilot said helpfully. "It's all covered by insurance, you know."

"It's not the money I'm yapping about—it's time. Those instruments and generators can't be duplicated anywhere except on Tellus, and even there it's all special-order stuff—oh, damn!"

CHAPTER THREE
"CLEAR ETHER!"

During the following days Tellurian Pharmaceuticals entertained Cloud. Not insistently—Graves was an expert in such matters—but simply by letting him know that the planet was his. He could do anything he pleased; he could have any number of companions to help him do it. And as a result he did—within limits—exactly what Graves wanted him to do. In spite of the fact that he did not want to enjoy life, he liked it.

One evening, however, he refused to play a slot machine, explaining to his laughing companion that the laws of chance were pretty thoroughly shackled in such mechanisms—and the idle remark backfired. What was the mathematical probability that all the things that had happened to him could have happened by pure chance?

That night he analyzed his data and found that the probability was an infinitesimal. And there were too many other incidents—all contributory. Six of them—seven if he counted his arm. If it had been his left arm—jet back! Since he wrote with his right hand, very few people knew that he was left-handed, and anyway, it didn't make any difference. Everybody knew that it took both hands and both feet to do what he did. Seven it was; and that made it virtually certain that accident was out.

But, if he was being delayed and hampered deliberately, who was doing it, and why? It didn't make any kind of sense. Nevertheless, the idea would not down.

He was a trained observer and an analyst second to none. Therefore he soon found out that he was being shadowed, but he could not get any truly significant leads.

"Graves, have you got a spy-ray detector?" he asked boldly—and watchfully.

The fat man did not turn a hair. "No, nobody would want to spy on me. Why?"

"I feel jumpy, as though somebody were walking on my grave. I don't know why anybody would be spying on me, but—I'm neither a Lensman nor an esper, but I'd swear that somebody's peeking over my shoulder half the time. I think I'll go over to the Patrol station and borrow one."

"Nerves, my boy, nerves and shock," Graves diagnosed. "Losing an arm would shock hell out of anybody's nervous system, I'd say. Maybe the Phillips treatment—the new one growing on—pulls you out of shape."

"Could be," Cloud assented moodily. His act had been a flop. If Graves knew anything—and he'd be damned if he could see any grounds for such a suspicion—he hadn't given away a thing.

Nevertheless, the Blaster went next to the Patrol office, which was of course completely and permanently shielded. There he borrowed the detector and asked the lieutenant in charge to get a special report from the Patrol upon the alleged gems and what, if anything, it knew about either the cruiser or the pirates. To justify the request he had to explain his suspicions.

After the messages had been sent the young officer drummed thoughtfully upon his desk. "Wish I could do something, Doctor Cloud, but I can't see how I can," he decided finally. "I'll notify Narcotics right away, of course, but without a shred of evidence I can't act, even if they are as big a zwilnik outfit as Wembleson's was, on Bronseca...."

"I know. I'm not accusing them. It may be anything from Vandemar to Andromeda. All firms—all individuals, for that matter—have spy-ray blocks. Call me, will you, when you get that report?"

The call came eventually and the Patrolman was round-eyed as he imparted the information that, as far as anyone could discover, there had been no Lonabarian gems and the rescuing cruiser had not been a Patrol vessel at all. Cloud was not surprised.

"I thought so," he said, flatly. "This is a hell of a thing to say, but it now becomes a virtual certainty—mathematically, the probability approaches absolute certainty as a limit—that this whole fantastic procedure was designed solely to keep me from analyzing and blowing out that vortex. Here's what I'm going to do." Bending over the desk, even in that ultra-shielded office, he whispered busily for minutes.

"But listen, Doctor!" the Patrolman protested. "Wait—let a Lensman do it. Do you realize that if they're clean and if they catch you at it, nothing in the universe can keep you from doing at least ninety days in the clink?"

"Yes. But if we wait, the chances are that it'll be too late. They will have had time to cover up whatever they're doing. What I am asking you is—will you back my play if I catch them with the goods?"

"Yes. We'll be here, armored and ready. But I still think you're completely nuts."

"Maybe so, but if my mathematics is wrong, it is still a fact that my arm will grow back on just as fast in clink as anywhere else. Clear ether, Lieutenant—until tonight."

Cloud made an engagement for luncheon with Graves. Arriving a few minutes early, he was of course shown into the private office. Seeing that the manager was busily signing papers, he strolled aimlessly to the side window and seemed to gaze appreciatively at the masses of gorgeously-blooming flowers just outside. What he really saw, however, was his detector. Since he was wearing it openly upon his wrist, he knew that he was not under observation. Nobody knew that he had in his sleeve a couple of small but highly efficient implements. Nobody knew that he was left-handed. Nobody knew that he had surveyed, inch by inch, the burglar-alarm wiring of this particular window, nor that he was an expert in such matters. Therefore no one saw what he did, nor was any signal given that he did anything at all.

That same night, however, that window opened alarmlessly to his deft touch. That side was dark, but enough light came through the front windows so that he could see what he was doing. Bad or good? He did not know. Those walls might very well have eyes, but he had to take that chance. One thing was in his favor: no matter how crooked they were they couldn't keep armored troops on duty as night-watchmen. That would be begging for trouble. And, in a pinch, he could get the Patrolmen there as fast as they could get their thugs.

He had not brought any weapons. If he was wrong, he would have no need of one and it would only aggravate his offense. If right, one wouldn't be enough and there would be plenty available. There they were, a drawerful of them. DeLameters—full charged and ready—complete with belts. He was right.

He leaped to Graves' desk. A spy-ray. That basement—"private laboratories"—was still blocked. He threw switch after switch—no soap. Communicators—He was getting somewhere now—a steel-lined room, a girl and a boy.

"Eureka! Good evening, folks."

It had not taken long for Ryder to arrive at the explanations of the predicament in which he and the girl were so hopelessly enmeshed.

"Thionite!" he explained to her, bitterly. "I never saw a man take thionite before, let alone die of it, but it's the only thing I can think of that can turn a man into such an utter maniac as that one was. They're *growing* the stuff. They must be a zwilnik outfit from top to bottom. That's why they've got to rub us out."

"But how could it get out?"

"Through a fault, Fairchild said, a crack in the rocks. A millionth of a gram is enough, you know, and the stuff's so fine that it's terrifically hard to hold. If we could only tell the Patrol!"

But they could not tell, nor could they escape. They exerted their every resource, exhausted every possibility—in vain. And as day followed day Ryder almost went mad under the grinding thought that they both must die without any opportunity of revealing their all-important knowledge. Hence he burst out violently when the death-cell's speaker gave tongue.

"Eureka? Damn your gloating soul to hell, Graves!" he yelled furiously.

"This isn't Graves!" the speaker snapped. "Cloud. Storm Cloud, the Vortex Blaster, investigating—"

"Oh, Bob, it is! I recognize his voice!" the girl screamed.

"Quiet! This is a zwilnik outfit, isn't it?"

"I'll say it is," Ryder gasped in relief. "Thionite—"

"That's enough, details later. Keep still a minute!" Locked together in almost overpowering relief, the imprisoned pair listened as the crisp voice went on:

"Lieutenant? I was right—zwilnik. *Thionite!* Get over here fast. Blast down the Mayner Street door—stairway on right, two flights down, corridor to left, half-way along left side, Room B twelve. Snap it up!"

"But wait, Cloud, wait!" they heard a fainter voice protest. "Wait until we get there. You can't do anything alone!"

"Can't wait. Got to get these kids out—evidence!" Cloud broke the circuit and, as rapidly as his one hand permitted, buckled gun-belts around himself. He knew that Graves would have to kill those two youngsters if he possibly could. If they were silenced, it was eminently possible that all other evidence could be destroyed in time.

"For God's sake save Jackie anyway!" Ryder prayed. He knew just how high those stakes were. "And watch out for gas, radiations, and traps—a dozen alarms must have been sprung before now all around here."

"What kind of traps?" Cloud demanded.

"Deadfalls, sliding doors—I don't know what they haven't got in this damned place."

"Take Fairchild's private elevator, Doctor!" the girl's clear voice broke in. "Graves said that he could kill us in here with gas or rays or—"

"Where is it?"

"The one farthest from the stairs."

Cloud jumped up, listening with half an ear to the babblings from below as he searched for air-helmets. Radiations, in that metal-lined room, were out—except possibly for a few narrow-beam projectors, which he could deal with easily enough. Gas, however, was bad. They couldn't weld cover-plates everywhere, even if they had time and metal. Every drug house had air-helmets, though, and this one must have hundreds of them. Ah! here they were!

He put one on, and made awkward shift to drape two more around his neck. He had to keep his one hand free. To the indicated elevator he dashed. Down two floors. He ran along the corridor and drove the narrowest, hottest possible cutting beam of his DeLameter into the lock of Room B Twelve. It took time to cut even that small semi-circle in that refractory and conductive alloy—altogether too much time—but the kids would know who it was. The zwilniks would unlock the cell with a key, not a torch.

They knew. When Cloud kicked the door open they fell upon him eagerly.

"A helmet and a DeLameter apiece. Get them on quick. Now help me buckle this—thanks. Miss Jackie, stay back there, clear of our feet. You, man, lie down here in the doorway. Keep your ray-gun outside, and stick your head out just barely far enough to see—no farther."

A spot of light appeared in a port, then another. Cloud's weapon flamed briefly. "I thought so. They do their serious radiation work somewhere else. The air right now, though, I imagine, is bad. It won't be long now. Do I hear something?"

"Somebody's coming, but suppose it's the Patrol?"

"They'll be in armor, so a few blasts won't hurt 'em. Maybe the zwilniks will be in armor, too—if so we'll have to duck—but I imagine that they'll throw the first ones in here just as they are."

They did. Graves, or whoever was directing things, rushed his nearest guards into action, hoping to reach B Twelve before anyone else could.

But as that first detachment rounded the corner Cloud's DeLameter flamed white, followed quickly by Ryder's, and in those withering blasts of energy the zwilniks died. The respite was, however, short. The next men to arrive wore armor against which the DeLameters raved in vain, but only for a second.

"Back!" Cloud ordered, and swung the heavy door as the attackers' beams swept past. It could not be locked, but it could be welded solidly to the jamb, which operation was done with dispatch, if not with neatness.

"I hope they come in time." The girl's low voice carried a prayer. Was this brief flare of hope false—would not only she and her Bob, but also their would-be savior die? "That other noise—suppose that's the Patrol?"

It was not really a noise—the cell was sound-proof—it was an occasional jarring vibration of the entire structure.

"I wouldn't wonder." Cloud looked around the room as he spoke. "Heavy stuff—semi-portables, perhaps. Well, let's see if we can't find some more junk like that trap-door to stick onto that patchwork. Jackie, you might grab that bucket and throw water. Every little bit helps and it's getting mighty hot. Careful! Don't scald yourself."

The heavy metal of the door was bright-to-dull red over half its area and that area was spreading rapidly. The air of the room grew hot and hotter. Bursts of live steam billowed out and, condensing, fogged the helmets and made the atmosphere even more oppressive.

The glowing metal dulled, brightened, dulled. The prisoners could only guess at the intensity of the battle being waged without. They could follow its progress only by the ever-shifting temperature of the barrier which the zwilniks were so suicidally determined to beam down. Then a blast of bitterly cold air roared from the ventilator, clearing away the gas in seconds, and the speaker came to life.

"Good work, Cloud and you other two," it said chattily. "Glad to see that you're all on deck. The boys have been working on what's left of the air-conditioner, so now we can cool you off a little and I can see what goes on there. Get into this corner over here, so that they can't blast you if they hole through."

The barrier grew hotter, flamed fiercely white. A narrow pencil of energy came sizzlingly through—but only for seconds. It expired. Through the hole there poured the reflection of a beam so brilliant as to pale the noonday sun. The portal cooled; heavy streams of water hissed and steamed. Warm water—almost hot—spurted into and began to fill the room. A cutting torch, water-cooled and carefully operated now, sliced away the upper two-thirds of the fused and battered door. The grotesquely-armored lieutenant peered in.

"Anybody hurt, Cloud?" he shouted. Upon being assured that no one was, he went on: "Good. We'll have to carry you out. Step up here where we can get hold of you."

"I'll walk and I'll carry Jackie myself," Ryder protested, while two of the armored warriors were draping Cloud tastefully around the helmet of a third.

"You'll get boiled to the hips if you try it. The water's deep and hot. Come on!"

The slowly rising water was steaming sullenly; the walls and the ceiling of the corridor gave mute but eloquent testimony of the appalling forces which had been unleashed. Wood, plastic, concrete, metal—nothing was as it had been. Cavities yawned; plates and pilasters were warped, crumbled, fused into hellish stalactites; mighty girders hung awry. In places complete collapse had necessitated the blasting out of detours.

Through the wreckage of what had been a magnificent building the cavalcade made its way, but when the open air was reached the three rescued ones were not left to their own desires. Instead, they were escorted by a full platoon of Patrolmen to an armored car, which was in turn escorted to the Patrol Station.

"I'm afraid to take chances with you until we find out who is who and what is what around here," the young commander explained. "The Lensmen will be here, with reinforcements, in the morning, but I think you had better stay here with us for a while, don't you?"

"Protective custody, eh?" Cloud grinned. "I don't remember ever having been arrested in such a nice way before, but it's QX with me. Thanks, Lieutenant, for everything."

Lensmen came, and companies of Patrolmen equipped in many and various fashions, but it was several weeks before the situation was entirely under control. Then Ellington—Councillor Ellington, the old Unattached Lensmen who was in charge of all Narcotics work—called the three detainees into the office which had been set aside for his use.

"We can release you now," the Lensman smiled. "Thanks, from me as well as from the Patrol, for everything you have done. There has been some talk that you two youngsters have been contemplating a honeymoon upon Chickladoria or thereabouts?"

"Oh, no, sir—that is—That was just talk, sir." Both spoke at once.

"I realize that the report may have been exaggerated or premature, or both, but it strikes me as being a sound idea. Therefore, not as a reward, but in appreciation, the Patrol will be very glad to have you as its guests throughout such a trip—all expense—if you like."

They liked.

"Very well. Lieutenant, take Miss Cochran and Mr. Ryder to the Disbursing Office, please.... Dr. Cloud, the Patrol will take cognizance of what you have done. In the meantime, however, I would like to say that in uncovering this attempt to grow Trenconian broad-leaf here, you have been of immense, of immeasurable assistance to us."

"Nothing much, sir, I'm afraid. I shudder to think of what's coming. If the zwilniks can grow that stuff anywhere—"

"Not at all, not at all," Ellington interrupted briskly. "No worse than ever, if as bad. For if such an entirely unsuspected firm as Tellurian Pharmaceuticals, with all their elaborate preparations and precautions—some of the inspectors must have been corrupted too, although we aren't to the bottom of that phase yet—could not get more than started, it is not probable that any other attempt will prove markedly successful. And in the case of the other habit-forming drugs, which Tellurian Pharmaceuticals and undoubtedly many other supposedly reputable firms have been distributing in quantity, you have given us a very potent weapon."

"What weapon?" Cloud was frankly puzzled.

"Statistical analysis and correlation of apparently unrelated indices—as you pointed out."

"But they have been used for years!" the Blaster protested.

"Admitted—but only when individual departures from the norm became so marked as to call for a special investigation. We now have a corps of analysts applying them as routine. Thus, while we cannot count upon having any more such extraordinary help as you have given us, we should not need it. I don't suppose that I can give you a lift back to Tellus?"

"I don't think so, thanks. My new flitter is en route here now. I'll have to analyze this vortex anyway. Not that I think it's abnormal in any way—those were undoubtedly murders, not vortex casualties at all—but just to complete the record. And since I can't do any extinguishing until I grow a new flipper, I might as well stay here and keep on practising."

"Practising? Practising what?"

"Gun-slinging—the lightning draw. I intend to get at least a lunch while the next pirate who pulls a DeLameter on me is getting a square meal."

9 789362 927330